# Rural Astronomy

*POEMS*

Georgann Eubanks

# Rural Astronomy

## Georgann Eubanks



ISBN  978-1-958094-57-0

POETRY

| | |
|---|---|
| BOOK DESIGN | EK Larken |
| COVER DESIGN | Davin Malasarn |
| COVER PAINTING | Georgann Eubanks |
| AUTHOR PHOTO | Donna Campbell |



PUBLISHED IN THE UNITED STATES OF AMERICA BY

EASTOVER PRESS
Rochester, Massachusetts
www.EastOverPress.com

For Donna,
who always gets the picture

# Contents

## II.

# Rural Astronomy

# The River Drew New Lines

"I could understand losing everything if this was a natural disaster, but a lot of this was
    a man disaster."     —Dorothy Cooper, flood survivor, Princeville, North Carolina

As the waters first began to rise, we learned that hogs' hooves,
like ladies heels, are too prim and slick to stand on tin.
Cows heavy with milk can't swim.
But chickens will bob to the top of their pens,
feathers pressed by wire in octagonal patterns.

When coffins rose and floated to town,
business did not improve.
Storefronts became aquariums
where new shoes swirled and danced,
then kicked out the lights.

Largemouth bass and perch rushed into a school,
passing their portraits on a science lab wall.
A globe twirled in the torrent while books,
launched from library shelves,
drifted down and opened like sea fans.

In the post office, junk mail grew heavier.
Outside, a Cadillac bumper clung to a juniper.
A Barcalounger found refuge in the limbs
of an oak before it broke and toppled.
In the slop and swill, the magnolias drowned more slowly.

When the water began to recede,
tires were cast across dead grass like black lifesavers.
Peanuts and pines began to brown.
When we plowed again, we turned up bottles and clothes
and recalled all that we had owned and loved.

# I.

## Coin Operated Scenic Viewer: *found poem*

Bring distant
points of interest
within close range
with the use of this
machine. For best
results, remove
eyeglasses. To clear
vision, turn red
knob. Quarters only.

Women's Work

In the photo,
the bass are fat as loaves.
Dad has one end of the stringer,
Bomer holds the other,
his mouth partway open.
Straw hats shade their blissful eyes.

What we don't see
are Ruby, Stella, Doris, and Kate
chopping the cabbage,
setting out plates,
stirring meal, buttermilk, and eggs—
while feeding the misery
of a woodstove in August,
the deep grease only
beginning to smoke.

# Terminal Birds

The sparrows in O'Hare
race above the moving walk,
circle and flutter down
to land in pairs at Gate B4.

Farther down at B1,
a lone male needles the carpet,
pecking for remnants of scones, pretzels,
Big Mac buns, and fries.

The birds seem unaware
of the world outside.
They have no desire to take
off toward that ridge of runway oaks.

The scraps here are plentiful,
the lights bright,
so much color to navigate,
so many possible destinations.

# Early Gender Studies

This morning,
two jays in the yard
one on the garden fence
the other on a limb more distant.

Each identical,
a painter's study,
the full spectrum of blue,
from winter ice
to lucent sapphire
to midnight navy.

A whole day and night's
worth of sky repeated
in lapping feathers,
neither bird duller than the other.
Which is male? Which female?

## Excursion

Bomer babied his '51 Pontiac Eight,
black and round as a hard-shell beetle.

The pleated seats were yellow vinyl.
A silver circle triggered the horn.

One day he took a notion to drive us
to Birmingham to visit his sister Ethel.

Stella hurried, packed pimiento cheese for me,
peanut butter crackers for her.

Bomer took a sleeve of saltines and a tin of sardines,
though he would never eat while driving.

Influenza orphans, they were farmed out.
Ethel to Aunt Lem, near blind, never strict.

Bomer got the short stick, raised by a grown
cousin who fed him after the beagles.

We drove toward afternoon sun, Stella dabbing
at Bomer's wet temple with her gloved hand.

To Stella, that car seemed a two-ton puzzle,
a man's machine. How would she change a tire,

master the stem shift, toe the clutch, or set the brake?
The steering wheel was scalloped for bigger fingers.

I fell asleep before we crossed into Alabama,
and woke being lifted by my armpits—

bare legs peeled from vinyl, like taffy
freed from wax paper, my Sunday dress damp at the neck.

We spread our picnic quick a mile before Ethel's house.
Bomer said he'd never tried her cooking.

## Counting Change

In the nineteen fifties,
a few minorities still jingled
in men's pockets:
Miss Liberty, Lady Justice,
the buffalo, bald eagle, and two Indians,
plus Mercury, that fleet Greek
and curious cross-dresser.

When Watts and bras started to burn,
the white men stopped minting
mythic women, Native Americans,
and endangered species.

To cover, they fashioned Susan B,
but made her too small,
reminding us of our
diminishment by inflation.
Then Susan, too, was cast out of circulation,
no more than a collector's item.

In the nineties
we came to understand
that Lady Justice is differently-abled,
while Ms. Liberty begins to look
suspiciously butch—those heavy calves,
her big hands bearing the frozen torch.
Still, she's barefoot and marooned
where teeming masses arrive
by ferry to look up her skirt.

# The Quarry

At five, I sit as directed
on the back porch slab,
a cool concrete seat,
the sweet gums fanning
sunlight from above.

I hold the end of a long string
tied to a stick that props up
an open box topped with screen wire,
a lean-to baited
with bread underneath.

Wrens and sparrows flee
when the jay comes to feed—
blue giant fussing, ill-tempered,
self important—impatient driver
in morning bird traffic.

With each hop toward the bait
the jay is resolute, defiant,
breast jutting, neck sharply
pivoting, observing me
with bullet eyes.

As instructed, once
the bird pecks bread,
I pull the string.
The trap sings down.
The trees above empty.

Now only the desperate
knock of wings. Tips of blue
feathers lick the wire like flames
on the gas stove where
Bomer's coffee still warms.

I call to him, never leaving
my quarry, as he pounds
across the screen porch
grabs his gloves on the sill—
those two perfect ghosts of his fingers.

In a magician's flurry of hands
he raises the trap,
unlodges the jay,
holds it firm,
a fist of throbbing feathers.

Then, right hand leading,
one sharp twist of the bird's blue
collar, a motion as rote
as my grandmother Stella,
snapping beans for supper.

Bomer pats my head with one hand,
holds the limp jay with the other.
"Good girl," he says.
"This boy won't rob my robins
or eat my bluebird eggs."

As other birds return,
I follow Bomer to the silver
can where we smell
yesterday's coffee grounds,
rank chicken skins,
and broken eggshells.

In mind I hear the preacher's words,
*the quick and the dead,*
and turn away at the thud
of the bird on the pile,
the clang of the can lid snapping shut.

# Vertigo

1

I'm a passenger in a parked car,
reading a magazine outside a drugstore.
A truck pulls in beside me, and for a moment
I have the sensation of rolling backwards,
brakes slipping.

2

Outside my bedroom window, the half-moon
is an upturned cup—white, empty,
and cold as predicted snow.
On the radio, an astronomer explains
that if we could anchor the moon,
earth could catch it in three hours flat.

3

The house of my childhood
floats down the street in a rainstorm,
buoyed between curbs,
shooting under an arch of trees.
I observe the journey from the den window.
The house stops for a red light.

4

Last night, again. This time a log cabin
is descending mountain trails, bumping oaks,
slinging itself into and out of
open fields, like a ride at the fair.
Just before I wake, I know it's not true.
I am fixed; it's all else that moves.

# No More Tears

While my parents
danced at the Shrine Temple,
I played the daughter
my aunt never had.

People often asked, "Is she yours?"
She'd say yes, and I would nod.
I had her cheekbones, and she
had my father's temper.

That night she drew me away
from Lawrence Welk's bubbles,
and we tangoed from the den
to her tiny kitchen.

She stood me on a chair,
rolled my collar under,
showed me how to bend
head-first into her sink.

The icy white porcelain
was gritty with Comet,
and now she aimed
to scour me.

I closed my eyes to conjure
a pearl drifting through
green goo—the Prell
shampoo we'd seen on TV.

She rolled up her billowing sleeves
to the roar of warming water. I sucked air,
smelling the bar of Ivory she kept
handy on its bed of plastic nails.

She drew the nozzle from its holster
and blasted—first warm, then hot,
then the ooze of baby shampoo.
Lather. Rinse. Repeat.

I heard her say "scalp," thinking TV Indians.
I dripped, my ears still roaring,
while she found another bottle—
White Rain—so I would smell like her.

At last with a towel sweet from Cheer
and rough from Wednesday's wind,
she swabbed my ears, tapped my bottom,
and twisted the towel into a turban.

Grateful to stand straight,
I waited while she found a comb.
Coming back, she pecked like a bird
at the mirror of my cheek.

## My Brother's Snake

Dad taught you how
to handle fear:
first by the neck,
then two handed,
to steady the tail.

Eventually you let her
slide through a belt loop
and rest on your leg while
we observed more closely—

her checkered belly,
rubber band tongue,
smell of musk,
that mock rattle.

In the aquarium
beside your bed,
the hognose
shed five times.

Once, we watched
her turn inside out
like our grandmother
peeling a stocking
and leaving it behind—
the wrinkled accordion
of a long day.

In the end,
you turned her
loose at the creek
her snout swollen
with a bite from
her own breakfast—
a pet store pinkie mouse
with the will to fight.

Three Word Signs: *found poem*

Minnows Worms Crickets
God Is Able
Guaranteed Credit Approval
Emergency Vehicle Entering
We Change Lives
Beware Sudden Icing
Thunder Cycles Open
Santos Woodcarving Popsicles
Support Our Troops
End Road Work
Death In Family
Sweet Corn Ahead
Tanningbeds Taxidermy Nightcrawlers

# Mountain Dawn

It tops the white pine first
like a brush dipped
in cadmium yellow, then
feathers the pines,
midriff, down the hill.

Later, a band of pink light
lines the ridge a mile west.
Close-by maple and ash drip
from last night's rumble and wash.

A mule brays from the hollow.
In three days, July will be gone.

# Sweet Potato Harvest

I was six when Bomer let me
help him clear the patch
on the far side of the pond—
a quarter acre beside the scuppernongs
that finally went soft
and sweet about the same time
he did that last year.

He turned the earth completely
over, never wounding a one,
while I loaded the wheelbarrow,
gently lifting every hobbled tuber
like the unwashed feet
of a whole Bible's worth
of lame children seeking cure.

When we finished,
I shouldered his hoe
and he rolled them home,
both of us silent as we crossed
the dam and climbed the path
to park our harvest
by the back porch stoop.

"Now, yams are for Yankees,"
he said, hosing them down.
"Our kind you just bake
till the skin withers,
and where the fork has pricked,
they'll ooze a sticky tar
that tells you they're done."

Then he grinned and stamped
the dirt from his boots.
"Nothing but old roots,"
he said. "But they keep."

# Flight Path

Across the sky the corridor
stretches: altitude's invisible
tube where jets streak south,
flying by satellite
toward home.

Their white trails are
first steady and straight
as grade school chalk,
then widen in wind,
edges erratic.

I watch the plumes loosen,
then nap until my fists,
tucked under,
grow numb
without blood.

I roll on my back,
hands useless,
fingers clawed
like my father's
after his stroke.

I imagine paralysis,
his condition
inherited, until
my fingers tingle
and eyes open,

I witness another
streak, bone white,
unspooling wide:
an X-rayed spine
crossing sun.

# Pouring the Slab

The do-it-yourself father unknots
the garden hose and pulls on gloves.

In the sun, his daughter
warms on her sawhorse perch,

wishing she could ride the red
wheelbarrow already loaded with her

playground sand. He rips a heavy sack
to pour a cloud of lime and clay.

The two-eyed hoe rasps
against the wheelbarrow's belly,

cement sifting with sand until a head
rises, the baby doll she'd buried there.

He adds water over and over as
the mixture swallows the hoe blade to hilt.

His bare arms thicken when he rolls the barrow,
and tips the lip to shake his mix into the frame

he nailed. A bed without a mattress,
this wood and rebar, the box filling

like a cake soon troweled smooth.
He calls her to him, engraves the date

with a stick, then presses her hand
to the slab, her small fingers under his,

the wet foundation cool, already hardening.

# Okra

On early summer stalks,
their parasols unfurl,
purple hearts in pools
of cream—a silken shade
to mask the nubs from sun.

Then circumcised by wind,
the blossoms drop and
furred spikes green—
at first, finger length and tender,
best picked before they harden.

Once plucked, boiled whole,
they defy the spoon, limp
as tongues and slick,
now slender mother fish,
their bellies bearing roe.

Cut to fry, each wheel
becomes a pistol chamber—
white bullet eggs loaded
in skin that purples again
in the last high heat
of the season.

# Siege

Under my mother's broom
whole divisions of thousand-legs
lost their ground while
every new squadron of sky
writers dropped, dangling
from mangled webs.

The wasps' paper tents
fell from the eaves
long before the legions
could properly honor their queen.

And in the cellar,
the patrol most lethal,
the skittering scorpions—
with their poison rockets
poised to launch—
surrendered in a crackle
beneath my father's boots.

Only the droning masons survived,
those black-winged daubers
hollowing flutes from Georgia red—
one clay spine welded to the next
until a whole pipe organ
hung across the carport wall.

My father said their flutes
were too high pitched
for us to hear. They trilled at
night as we dreamed, at first
an elegant dirge, mourning the lost,
and then a reveille calling all
living creatures back to battle
and drill against our encampment.
He never took a hammer to them.

## Summer Departing

Before the curtain of fog pulls back,
a patter of chill rain moistens
bird feathers and mutes the katydids.

The titmouse laughs like an old smoker,
a distant wren pleads for brighter light,
the junco shakes a limb, and yellow leaves drop.

Fewer swallowtails come
to sip at milkweed now.
Cosmos is drooping.
Yarrow and sedum still bloom.

At last the sun scales the roof,
warming the yard with light.
The tin roof ticks and hummingbirds
resume their skirmishes.

Colors deepen, tiny globes
of water swell, catch light
and drop this last morning
of solvent August.

# College Town Chauffeur

The robin is a fledge, still molting and vocal.
She sits in the myrtle until we come near,
then fusses and drops to the side mirror of a blue VW
parked in the yard of a student rental.

She gurgles and, with one hard bat of wings,
levitates to the roof rack—a solid perch
where she preens and barks—
warning us not to come nearer.

For a week she is there each morning
as I walk the dog, and in that odd robin way
of dipping head and evil eye, she appraises me and my dog,
as if we might have a way to lead her blue mother away.

The day before summer begins, the student yard is empty.
No car. Graduation has come and gone.
I look for the robin up the block, but only a showy
gang of cardinals struts the black top.

Next day, the old bug is back, washed and waxed.
Sure enough, the robin is there, stirring the myrtle.
She flies to the driver's window, her bold eye never leaving
me as she pecks at the chrome, wanders the windshield.

When she rises to the roof, I see she has taken on
more color—redder breast, darker wings,
her early feathers shed. She has earned her license,
fully prepared to drive us away.

## Motel Soaps

Third drawer down,
beside the red enema bulb
and Dad's old shaver,
the topless shoebox
was full of them:
Sweetheart, Camay,
and Cashmere Bouquet.

He brought them home
from business trips,
souvenirs of one-motel
towns with names like
Lavonia, Toccoa,
Homer, and Unicoi.

Saturday nights he'd give
me a fresh cake to shuck
while my mother tested the water.
I'd sniff the perfume and trace
the pink lady in relief
and her embossed bouquet.

With the slide of those bars
I learned my own skin,
traveled every tuck and knoll
until a wafer, soft and near-melted,
had bent to the shape of my palm.

After the divorce, week by week,
she would open a new bar,
set it by the guest bath sink,
so all could have a hand
in dissolving the ladies
and their bouquets.

## Stunt Man

The middle-aged man in a T-shirt, jeans, and circus slippers
toes a steel cable strung across the Grand Canyon.
He dips the balance pole, angled like the hands of a clock.
Ragged wind puffs up his pants, swirls his thinning hair,
flattens the T-shirt against his American belly.

Wired for the world to hear, he speaks without ceasing:
*Praise the Lord and won't You please calm these winds?*
*Do it, Lord, you have the power now. Yes, Lord, now.*
Thank God not all of us need such a chance
to believe in powers greater than ourselves.

Take the fisherman who shoves off in bitter dark,
watching the sky with a seasoned eye, ever vigilant
for squall lines, the mounting swells, the possible tangle
of lines and nets that could pull him overboard.
He glances at the TV acrobat as he leaves for the dock.

The ICU nurse is following ropes of light
on multiple monitors as if some divine cowboy
is slinging lassos to scare off rattlers.
She stops by the breakroom to catch his act.

The hard hat man is not watching, he lives it—
setting hot rivets with a welding torch
that could blind him if his mask flies off in sudden wind
or he loosens the lock of his thighs on a high beam.

Meanwhile, on the other side of the chasm,
a second camera pushes in on the wife and children,
holding their heads as if their hair might soar away.
*Please, Father,* they whisper.

The camera pans back to the wire. The tension tightens.
The stunt man is halfway, proclaiming his faith for millions
of dollars. This one-man parade will make news around the world—
as if daily gravity were not gamble enough.

## Her Cucumber Pickles

In August
still warm from sun
they gave up the vine.
She scrubbed their spurs
as jars chimed on the stove.

Laid by in the cellar,
those sacred green wheels
took up the salt, bathed
in the same sour gold
that crossed her Savior's lips.

Not until the New Year
would she let us loosen
a single ring, pry up
the Mason's seal with a pop
more festive than champagne.

We'd fork those coins,
fish out the pale eels of onion
and dots of mustard roe—
spread them like evening grace
over our steaming plates.

# The Pillar

And here is Lot,
the man who left
without looking back,
a hero of the ages
for those who despise
God's Others.

And here is
the nameless wife,
who turned her head,
still wondering
at the need for leaving.

Though he is revered,
she became the seasoning
in every kitchen—
the same taste
of blood in us all.

# Shad Fishing on the Trent River
*—for Walter Henderson*

March midnight under a full moon
and trail of stars, we take your pickup,
drive past young pines in rows as certain
as your father's plantings.

We park beside a steep bank to test
this tea-black river. I step in, my fingers
in your clean, chilled hand.
The canoe shudders.

You paddle, one-armed,
the spatulate end never leaving water,
stirring us silent, forward.
I shine the light.

We find the end or beginning. Which?
You pull. The net drops opals—
persimmon and turquoise—
rising sure as sun.

But the river water stops my shine
by inches only giving up brown like
beer glass, then closer gold
like whiskey.

There is new weight here. You say it
even before the first come tumbling up,
a cache of fresh coins, the scales
catching light like lenses.

There are three, then six, then ten.
A trickle of blood soon coils
between our feet, while the shad
thrash at the boat's bottom.

No spawning from these. Instead
a mingling: tomorrow's oil and corn meal,
the splatter and pop, skin crisp, flesh sweet,
only the bones tossed back.

# Sightseer

If you look back carefully
there's a good chance
that what you've become
is really what you've been all along.

Take me, for example.
It's not possible to say for certain
when I went from being an amateur
to a professional sightseer—

from dilettante to expert tourist.
I was in second grade when the guide
passed me his Eveready flashlight

deep inside a Tennessee mountain.
We'd already seen seven states that morning—
and now we were a knot of families in the dark

heading toward the so-called Ruby Falls.
I'd won the flashlight because I could explain
the difference between stalactite and stalagmite—

not much different in my child mind
from new teeth top and bottom
sprouting in my own mouth.

So began my fact collections and the first lure
of leading a group of strangers somewhere exotic,
even if falsely lit by ruby colored lights.

II.



At the Inn: *found poem*

Previous guests please note:
we now have air conditioning, Wi-Fi,
and the rooster has moved.

## Their Gardens

Now I am the keeper of the crabapples
along the roadside, the boxwoods that line
the drive, the azalea and camellia in
pine straw beds beside the tulip tree.

I am the keeper of liriope,
of ajuga in shade, the variegated acuba,
the snowball bush of boutonnieres,
caladiums nodding in boxes along the stoop.

I am the keeper of her clematis that climbs
the trellis beside the garage, the fragrant moon flowers
that cling to the screened porch siding,
and the bank of gardenias beyond.

I am the keeper of the hybrid tea roses in the full sun bed,
the coral honeysuckle that climbs by the pines,
his peach and plum trees that she would not spray,
the quince by the picnic table, the hydrangea and spirea.

I am the keeper of the necklace of poppies,
the daffodils that lined each ledge,
the horse tail near the basement door,
the sweet tea olives and summer begonia.

I am the keeper of the marigolds and pansies by the shed
that she started from seed, the sweet shrub and dogwood,
along the path to the pond, his gladiolas and dahlias
cultivated in rows, ready to cut for the Methodist altar.

I am the keeper of the catalpa and its caterpillars for bait,
the mulberries held in purple stained fingers,
the muscadine and scuppernong tunnel
beside the rows of sweet potatoes that he dug in fall.

I am the keeper of the daylilies, the bass and bream,
the tadpoles and bullfrogs bellowing in our dreams,
the lonely pear by the pond that always ripened late.

I am the keeper of my people and their plantings,
the land sold for mansions, the landscape memorized,
I am the last among the flourishing.

# Rural Astronomy

Tonight, the moon is a crock
pouring blue john through the skylight.
By April it bathes the bed.
Come May it pools on the floor.
By June I must rise and take
my face right up to the glass
to drink in the pearly angle of light.

So it is with the sun.
You learn in the Blue Ridge
to follow the march of light and shadow.
Note where Venus arrives at dusk.
Then the Dipper begins to drop,
retrieving water in a path so slow
that each night's movement is no more
than a single frame in a looping film.

# Redemption

*Spring*
Buckets of May rain in the Blue Ridge
have leafed out golden oak and ash.
A cold front roars in like the tide, rolls over treetops in waves.
Close your eyes and listen to this ocean.

*Summer*
Leaf ocean, dark green trees breathe,
full boughs sweep down, then up with tidal grace—
a slow, slanting motion like Tai chi.

*Autumn*
It's been a month since I've seen them.
Like maroon robed priests, they bless me.
Everything has changed. They nod, then wait.
I bow in return.

*Winter*
I can see every mountaintop,
islands beyond these gray weathered planks.
The deck of this cabin could be the prow of a ship.

Then, east to west, the hard wind sweeps in,
bare limbs wave, and for a moment I believe
this whole place has set sail.

# Snowbirds

September begins
with a persistent breeze,
leaves never still,
waving summer on
to the east,
hurrying the fall,
wearing down the already
yellow and spent.

The hummingbirds
are dazed pilots in training
for the long flight to Mexico.
The crabby old men—
those few who are left—
can feel it coming:
the day they must pack
the Cadillac or Tahoe,
drive their chatty wives to Florida,
open those musty quarters,
resume the Banlons and khaki shorts,
tanned knees bare and frowning
as they swat at pickleballs,
trying not to run.

## The Median

Six a.m. like so many fragile
mornings in ashen light
that echoes the gray
pavement before me, I clear
the last mountain, lower
the car through broad curves
in first traffic and last fog,
land on the flat stretch,
putting the miles back.

Then, like suddenly stirred
coals—taillights ahead—a choke
of cars and semis braking.
From the mist, the shape
clarifies, a horse the color
of dry blood steams
up the median, hooves crushing
weeds, her flanks quivering:
a dark archaic machine.

Each driver's heart
must drum with her run,
weighing any sudden turn,
not like interstate possum or dog
to be pummeled to raw mounds.
The horse forces us to crawl, imagine
the matted mane at windshield,
belly riding hood, her long bones
like pipe ramming our thin metal.

She passes, headed where I'd come,
safe only by traveling the divide.
As traffic thins, I lose her
in the mirror, still wondering
where the fence had broken,
what boundary had given in.
Could anyone know at this hour
she was already gone?

## Suet

After he died,
Stella kept the house
spare and neat.

Each day a ritual:
Wednesday wash,
Thursday shop,

Friday mow,
Saturday weed,
Sunday to church.

And so, it went—
predictable and smooth—
everything straight,

save for the nail
she'd driven slant
in the outside sill.

Below the picture window,
it was a promise
that come winter,

she'd stab a cube
of butcher's suet
there for her birds.

As direct winter light
turned the window
into mirror,

we'd wait—she
in his recliner, me
in a wingback chair.

Titmouse, nuthatch,
and downy pecked
at breakfast and left,

until at last,
the smallest bird,
the one most shy—

the ruby crowned kinglet—
took his chance, worried
over his shoulder,

then turned to catch
his own reflection—
the red feathered crown
rising like flames.

# Fall Day

Late afternoon at a turnout on the high desert road,
a station wagon empties on the slim shoulder—a mother
and her brood, three boys with rubber snakes in hand,
the very embodiment of boisterous.

The fourth child, the eldest, unfolds from the front,
stepping out in a dress, barefoot on cooling stones.
She crosses her bare arms, eyes set on a distant cliff.
It might have been a Rockwell scene.

But in northern New Mexico, yellow aspens quake
while the Virgin Mother watches from a flank of sandstone
in the red hills above. Her nicho is festooned with fading
plastic roses, her feet darkened by miraculous water.

If Adam and Eve had been children,
Adam would have been the first to put his hands
on the snake, and Eve, unhappy, feigning boredom,
would have refused any temptation to scream or run.

Likewise, this older sister keeps her cool,
while the boys dart and tease around her.
The mother, vexed, looks to the Virgin,
crosses herself, and settles again behind the wheel.

# Blue Ridge Motor Court

The young innkeeper
was born with a heart for hospitality.
He bought an old motel,
retiled each bath—
every five-inch square
re-grouted and replaced.

He landscaped the courtyard
with lilacs and honeysuckle
to scent the afternoons.
He planted annuals for color
and put in a burbling fountain
to sing his guests to sleep.

He mastered a recipe for
pecan and sour cream waffles,
fruit compote on the side.
He ordered strong coffees
from Ecuador, pillow
chocolates from Belgium.

Then the six-lane drowned out
his fountain and fouled the flowers
with diesel smoke and dust.
He came to resent the few guests he drew
and their plans for the next destination,
their life on the road.

## Resurrection Bay, Alaska

Better than a circus,
first comes the swimming bear,
making his way from cove to island.

Gray whales emerge,
racing us port and starboard—
vessels far sleeker than ours.

We snap our cameras and swoon,
and for a moment,
we are in their school.

As the boat drums on, the isle
of puffins comes close enough
to show us their colors.

Orange beaks and black caps,
they huddle like monks on the rocks.
They can fly at 400 wing beats per minute,

the captain claims on a loudspeaker.
They also swim with their wings
as if flying underwater.

Around the bend, nearer to shore,
sea lions lounge, ignoring our intrusion.
We admire their tender ways.

Turning back to deeper water,
as if on cue, a pair of orcas
breaks the surface.

A twain of tails and torsos,
they snort seawater, sudden
fountains that drown our engines.

Soon we fix on silver cliffs ahead
as the boat plows toward the deepest fjord—
ancient monuments of ice, history frozen.

The captain bids us not to speak, orders
full throttle, creates a mammoth wake,
then kills the engines. We hold silent.

There is only the rush of wind
before the cracking begins—
like lightning, then thunder.

In slow motion the glacier breaks,
crumbles, whole stories of ice
like vertebrae shatter and plunge.

Shards with blue hearts rise
on a mounting wake that rolls
toward us and slaps us back.

# Scuppernongs

In his garden
the vines writhed
naked through winter.
Then in heat they
put on leaves to hide
their gaudy baubles.

Not until fall
did they soften to confirm
our first temptation—
full-bellied and freckled,
near bursting to deliver
new meat, seed, and juice.

Baptist among grapes,
leather hulled
and quick to ferment,
they could make a wine
sweet enough to fill a head
with morning regret.

But shed of old skins
and sieved of seed,
the flesh boiled down
to be redeemed.
The jelly waits for winter
in the cellar.

# Third Wednesday in November

This is the hour
of the gale force gusts,
the forecaster says,
and already the lip
of the tin roof is snarling.

Limber oaks comb
through sideways snow
and a lone squirrel climbs
a mast of swaying pine
to scout for calmer seas.

When metal chairs
start to chatter and slide
toward the railing,
a startled wren shoots
to a new roost.

My job inside this vessel
is to keep the pipes warm,
punch at the fire, and pray
the power lines stay clear
until guests arrive to give thanks.

## Guessing Colors

The road had been dirt when they built the house.
Bomer dug the pond while Stella sewed yellow curtains.
They laughed–who would possibly peek in their windows?
Their only neighbors were buried in the new memorial park
a few miles up the road. "A real dead end," Bomer told her.

The road was finally paved by the time the last grandchild came.
More houses and new roads began to carve up the forest.
On the front porch stoop, Bomer would sit with the child
and they'd guess the color of the next car coming up the road.

Sometimes he'd bring a bag of M&M's, slit the corner
with his pocketknife so one candy could squeeze out at a time.
Between cars, they'd guess the candy colors–orange, brown,
green, yellow, red.  The correct guess got the treat.
They'd tongue the chocolate until it melted.

The game stopped when a slow string of cars,
the first one black, passed, each burning headlights.
Bomer knew it wouldn't be long before he took that ride himself,
under a saddle of fresh cut flowers, color depending on season.

Thirty more springs, Stella washed yellow pollen off the stoop
and near the end, she shared her house with a tomcat stray.
When all the grandchildren gathered, wearing their best for Stella,
they stood on the stoop, looking out, while traffic backed up
as the new light at the corner ran its cycle.
Green-yellow-red and back to green.

## The Attraction

Repairing the fence on the far side of the field, Charles
       discovered the special attraction that lightning had for him.

It came rolling along the barbed wire in a ball of blue,
          and Charles knew enough to run for his life.

That night, his father told him tales of farmers struck,
        their hoe handles smoking, black, the blades curling.

Others found melted coins
          or a pocket watch exploded in their overalls.

One man from the flatlands, alone in bed and not
        a cloud he could see, was struck through the window.

The bedsprings were twisted, a black hole in the sheets,
            but he lived to tell it.

As a grown man, Charles could drive with friends
          in an easy rain along a slow river,

and the bolts would fork down,
        light and sound at once, to remind him.

Whenever the clouds began to boil, Charles knew to seek shelter,
       and check for rods on rooftops when he visited kin.

Now, at seventy, Charles's heart is irregular. His wife insists
       they carry the heart starter wherever they go.

All night it flashes white, like distant lightning, charged and ready
     inside the cloth bag with the red cross, close beside the bed.

# Cooter Pie

Bomer Henry's childhood tastes
ran from squirrel to frog,
so when he promised cooter pie,
his children squirmed.
Daddy, not turtle, too!

"Be thankful your father
is so resourceful. You
will swallow every bite,"
he said, eyeing Stella,
willing her silent
as he drew on gloves.

Down by the lake,
an orphaned boy again,
Bomer snared the snapper
quick with a chicken thigh
while tadpoles stirred the silt.

Meanwhile, Stella floured
the other chicken parts
and set a pot of snaps to boil,
just in case turtle or husband
proved too tough.

She often softened
his history lessons
with such compromise,
but it was she who took
a hammer to the shell
after he drove a nail to its brain.

The children cleaned their plates,
and the chicken sat cold.
Then Bomer told his orphan's tale again:
how you make a meal from what you catch.
Stella kept to herself how much
like Bomer the turtle was.

# City Symphony

At first light, outside my condo window
the cardinal in the holly
mimics the sound of scissors
trimming hair.

The snip snip is neither musical
nor patterned, more like a conductor's
rap on a podium, offering a downbeat
to the wrens who erupt in bold coloratura.

Next the maestro brings in the higher sparrows
who flute away until the nuthatch brass
builds the theme and a jay's French horn
calls all to feed.

When the air warms, a hawk cheers from high above,
her shadow reminds the players they are never safe.
So goes their day, trilling away in multiple
movements before the light's decrescendo.

# Snake Handler at the Writers' Conference
*—for Tim McLaurin*

The room steams,
rank with our mammalian heat,
gathering from all the slow
acts that have come before.

When you took the stage,
hauling the six-pack cooler
and the crook neck stick,
some poet ladies in the early rows
rose and grabbed their purses.

Face blank as paper, you knelt,
cocked the box lid, and hoisted out
what might have been a rope trick,
the way the king and hognose tangled.

Not the same danger as the venom
delivered by your doctors—
a chemo so strong it killed
a snake that bit you one night.

Now, at arm's length, your charges offer
their dangling message—no words, only punctuation.
Comma, slash, and question mark
that you shake free into separate, grateful exclamations.

## Congealed Salad

Every Christmas
another novel combination,
just like our dwindling family—
odd flavors of boxed gelatin
shot through with canned fruit,
marshmallows, cream cheese,
and pecans–concocted by my aunts
who always strayed from the recipe.

This variegated dome
flipped from the mold
and topped with a mayo star
was centerpiece among
the steaming bowls,
wreathed in green, slick
as Georgia marble and motionless,
at least through grace.

But once the turkey was stripped
and our dinner plates emptied,
every serving rode back
to the kitchen, none of us having
managed our wedge.
The wobbling portions
set out by the sink, each
weeping into its own lettuce bed.

# Mule Ear Chair

Hairy oak tendrils
hang from the underside
of this slat seat chair
and surprise my fingers.

The woven splits are new,
a repair that Anita
the antique dealer made.
Found in an abandoned mill,
she said. Seat sat plum out.

*Might've been one Woody
made, or his brother Arval,*
the mill man told her. Sold
them three-for-a-dollar
to peddlers who traveled the gaps.

The frame was turned
on a lathe, then planed
up top to mock a mule,
ears pinned back, caught
in a pose of suspicion.

Steam bent and tenon joined,
the legs sit low to the ground—
just right for the tail end
of a day to lean back
and study the stars.

## Molting

For years the skins have startled me,
shucked on a rock or the rough-hewn chestnut
under the eaves. This year's first was flung
like a luminous scarf over the shoulder
of the gutter, wispy and beckoning in a breeze.

Others have clung to the cabin like windsocks,
gauging the gales that cross the ridge, until a gust
blows them down. Once I found a ball of skin
rolled into itself near the bed of Lucifer lilies
where today the racer appeared.

He might have been a big man's belt
left out too long in weather,
beginning to crenellate after a winter
in the grass. But the periscope head
showed me I was being watched.

Despite the risk of visiting bears.
I'd laid out a banquet for the birds.
All day the fearless juncos had been feeding,
then a chipmunk, and a baffled squirrel.

I had gone inside to prepare dinner—
a red sauce and, of all things,
spaghetti di nero—not colored by squid ink,
but slick noodles made from black beans.

Hearing her growl, I came out
to find the dog chasing the chipmunk
who had enticed the snake
who froze in the grass
and pretended to be an errant cable,
driven to the ground in wind.

I snagged the dog who paused
at the worry in my voice.
I filled a pitcher and flung water
at the snake, who ducked
and then sipped at the droplets.
The sun surely hot on its back.

## White Cat

He knew his meals
by the scent and suck
of her canvas shoes,
the rasp of her hose like
a bath from his own tongue.

Stella moved slow, over oak
to carpet to linoleum,
then the whank
of the cabinet letting
loose, the hard tooth
biting metal, the crank
turning, giving back briny air.

She'd shrill his name, but he
was there, dragging his leg
with the inside pin, his one
mistake, that sudden car.

When she took up the cane,
the tip like a third rubber
shoe, tapping the floor,
he never shied,
but gave her more room.

The night she left, carried
on four rubber wheels,
rolling from their bed, he hid
under her sewing cabinet
until the house was still,
all the white-legged strangers
absent but for their scent.

A man came next
morning to let him out.
Her birds and chipmunks
were all he had left.
But he was too slow.
She had feared the very
same thing: a pin
in the hip and a cold
bowl from a foreign hand.

## Colonial Capital

The photos in this hotel are garish—
framed images of Tryon Palace
where colonials governed and are yet revered.
Today the guides are careful to say *first white men,*
but pride of possession is yet unchecked.

In one shot, the gilded statue of a true Native
rests on a pedestal, ossified, romanticized,
surrounded by a geometry of boxwoods,
fountains of azaleas, wilderness manicured.

No servants anywhere in sight,
only the results of their labors—
not an errant leaf on the walks,
every brick snug against the next.

This extravagant confection,
the region's biggest attraction,
was built on a swamp still sinking
in a morass of greed now gone abroad.

# Anthropomorphic

Suppose we had privileged the subtle:
the she-feathers with tones varied
as sandstone lit by first light.

We might have called them earthen birds instead of cardinal,
from which followed ecclesiastical princes, the adjective
for first order sin, and numbers fundamental to accounting.

Why did we revere the he-bird, garish as blood, lording
over the seed? Consider the little goldfinch, strutting
in his yellow epaulets. Even he cannot trump the painted bunting.

Yet what if this mother grosbeak, and not her rose-breasted mate,
had defined the species? Might she be called the brush-stroke
grosbeak for the play of umber and ivory around her eyes?

Only the birds whose coloring is the same across genders
are named for other features: the chickadee for its voice,
the tufted titmouse for its crest.

Don't blame Mother Nature for these boys dressed in drag,
or their wives wearing drab, not when humans decide
"laying an egg" also means a showy blunder.

*Lunaria*

Bomer laid rock from the back porch stoop to your flowering beds,
flagstone shapes like U.S. states wandering the yard.
I skipped from Georgia to Montana, calling capitals
learned from cards. You pointed out the girlish blooms–
peony, pansy, iris, quince—names of your grade school friends.

Morning of the funeral, I step each stone
through late June grass, listening to the finch and wren.
Beside your daylilies' trumpets, the money plant shudders,
its coins dried thin like parchment hung on brittle stems.
*Lunaria*, they whisper your Latin to me.

Seeded from these, deep purple they'd bloomed in my yard, too.
I pocket one oval to hold, fingering the fragile skin and stem.
Later, you seem just as light when we lower the box next to the stone
where years ago, your gloved hand held mine at Bomer's planting.

# Snarl

Hood to trunk
and door to door,
the cabs jockey,
rock, and honk—
a ribbon of yellow
raring back
and pitching forward
as lights change,
and cops whistle.

Trucks merge
from side streets,
tapping on horns,
hoping for
quick admission.

That was Monday in Manhattan.

Two days later,
on a narrow ferry
to a barrier island
in Carolina,
our cars are
in a tight row
hood to trunk,
and door to door.

My compact is
parked between
a Buick and
an outboard trawler
on a trailer.

Damn if
these fixed
vehicles with
blocks wedged
under tires
are now beeping
when passengers
abandon them,
locking doors
with Bluetooth fobs
and climbing
to the higher deck,
watching the squalls
roll toward us.

A black American
Standard Poodle
in the Subaru
behind me fidgets
in the driver's seat,
his narrow
nose barely above
the half-lowered window.
He leans on the horn
like a cabbie, impatient
for his next fare.

# Cabin Guest

As I open the drawer, looking
for an inch of cellophane tape,
why does a shriek fly out of me
as if I were teetering on a ledge
about to let go, falling to my death,
when it's only a mouse stirring awake?

Scrawny thing, you're barely
the size of a dust bunny.
Beady eyes and half asleep in a nest
of lamp wicks we never use
but keep should the power fail.

You and your kin log more days
in this cabin than I ever will,
gnawing the soap bar in the shower,
running winter races over
knives in the utensil drawer
like Marines on an obstacle course.

Every spring when we pull the sheets
off the daybed and rockers, dust off
the bookshelves and tables,
turn the mattresses, and reconnect
the washer and dryer, we find
your evidence broadcast like seeds.

I value your invisibility, hearing
only the muffled ticks at night
as you make your hopeful forays.
Far better than my laying out trays
of poison. Yet, when the dog catches scent
of you and will not be deterred, it unnerves me.

Today, when they came with the new
fridge and rolled the old one away,
your cousin was there, under the coils,
desiccated, still clinging like a gray
boll of cotton. She went without fanfare,
feet up, as will I one day.

## Major Medical Center

Ambulances unload at the last door.
Walk-ins wait at the valet station
to give up their keys for a wheelchair.
Two mockingbirds oversee this territory.

One bird hops through spokes of rubber wheels,
taking shelter under blue vinyl seats.
The other pecks at a wad of gauze on asphalt
and darts between traffic cones.

By midnight, the arrivals multiply—
shifts end, fevers flare, children squirm,
and waiting rooms fill with moaning
as the mockers rise to the power lines.

They mimic the harsh wail
of trucks backing up and higher beeps
that leak from car doors left open,
keys abandoned in ignitions.

By sunrise, though, they'll revert to Nature—
crow caw and sparrow trill, riff of cat, and wren song—
until another ambulance arrives, exhaust rising,
the gray breath of a new morning.

# The Neighbor Ladies Gather at a Safe Distance

The mourning doves flutter like gloved applause.
It is the first day of November.
They should be here any minute.
It looks colder than it is.

It is the first day of November.
They'll lower her oak today.
It looks colder than it is.
It would be better if the sun were shining.

They'll lower her oak today.
The heart of that tree went gradually hollow.
It would be better if the sun were shining.
So much in the center is totally rotten.

The heart of that tree went gradually hollow.
I would be afraid to climb it.
So much in the center is totally rotten.
She should have had it done sooner.

I would be afraid to climb it.
It could have fallen on any of us.
She should have had it done sooner.
She never comes out of that house.

It could have fallen on any of us.
Her yard is a disgrace.
She never comes out of that house.
The noise will drive us all indoors.

Her yard is a disgrace.
They should be here any minute.
The noise will drive us all indoors.
The mourning doves flutter like gloved applause.

# To Own a Place in the Mountains

It used to be when I visited these ridges,
climbed through spruce and huckleberry,
sniffed the skunk scent of galax,
marveled at the snowy trillium,
I ached for a patch to claim,
seized by such a longing,
hardly leaving room
for the present.

Now I have it, this sanctuary
of chestnut and chinking,
tin roof, stone chimney—
all quiet and mine,
at least for a time.

The longing comes now
when I am back in the flatlands
missing the hiss and snap
of burning locust, the risen moon,
treetops turning in gentle wind.

All I have in the city is the click
of a keyboard and screen, a virtual means
to take me anywhere but these deep woods
that now own me.

# Rural Electric Newsletter: *found poem*

*Available*

PSI Power washer
A-frame timberjack
Jersey cow in milk, she takes on orphan calves
6' Titan land plane leveler/grader–3 part hitch attach
Folding bicycle
Alpaca kerosene cooker
2010 Ford Escape tailgate, glass & bumper
Rare vintage cowboy coffee table w/ glass top
Corvette hoods
Blessing trumpet
Tennessee fainting goats, (3 males)


*Wanted*

Old barn to take down for materials
Caretaker for weekends
Someone to split & stack firewood
Goats, free or cheap

# Clawfoot Tub
*—for Liza Plaster*

This clawfoot tub is slow to fill.
I take turns mixing hot and cold
from separate faucets.

Chilled, I finally dip in, sit,
stretch out, my back against
cold, coated iron.

As the water surrounds my knees
it comes to me: these mountains
will grow shorter, as sea level rises.

I sink deeper, taking in the heat,
breathe healing vapors—
mint, lemon, and bergamot.

I know this earthy handmade soap
will cloud the water, but I take
the cloth and lather away.

On this foothills farm
the towels are line-dried.
They are thick and rough,
the sun yet woven in their fibers.

# The Last of It

On the last day
of the year,
of the century,
of the millennium,
we bought the last load
of locust, cherry, and oak
from a man of eighty
who drove a '66 Chevy
on bare tires, buying
five dollars' worth
of gas at a time.

He told us how he'd been
spared at Pearl Harbor,
how he was raised
on the rough side
of the mountain.

If you didn't can or cure it,
you didn't eat, he said.
And if he had a chance
to go around again,
he'd pass. Let the Lord
take him any day.
Once was gracious plenty.

Then, on that last evening,
of the century, wood stacked
and ready to warm us,
we stood on the ridge
watching the late sun bloom
and wilt like a Japanese flower.
Above, a downy woodpecker
tapped out a Morse Code message
that only our fathers
might have deciphered.

# ACKNOWLEDGMENTS

Thanks to Darnell Arnoult for her persistence, Denton Loving for his easy mentorship, and Jennifer Stewart Miller for her practical sense of thrifty language.

Thanks also to the editors of the following publications where versions of some of these poems first appeared: *Southern Review* ("The Median"); *Georgia Journal* ("Sweet Potato Harvest"); *Habersham Review* ("Siege" and "Flight Path"); *Salmon Magazine* ("Shad Fishing"); *Negative Capability* ("White Cat"); *Sandhills Review* ("Snake Handler at the Writers' Conference").

I am grateful to the entire EastOver team for their generous support and to the amazing Davin Malasarn for the cover typography and design. Special appreciation also goes to Scout Larken for care and guidance with the interior typography and design.

**GEORGANN EUBANKS** is a widely published writer, Emmy-winning documentarian, and popular speaker. She received an NC Arts Council Fellowship, was one of the four founders of the NC Writers Network and has served as chair of North Carolina Humanities, Arts North Carolina, and the NC Literary and Historical Society. She is director of the Table Rock Writers Workshop and the author of six books of non-fiction from the University of North Carolina Press. The latest is *The Fabulous Ordinary: Discovering the Natural Wonders of the Wild South.* She is director and literary executor of the Paul Green Foundation. *Rural Astronomy* is her first poetry collection.